EYE SEE UNITY

EYE SEE UNITY

Beautiful Art the Rose That Is She

Angela Butler

iUniverse, Inc.
Bloomington

EYE SEE UNITY
Beautiful Art the Rose That Is She

iUniverse books may be ordered through booksellers or by contacting:

iUniverse
1663 Liberty Drive
Bloomington, IN 47403
www.iuniverse.com
1-800-Authors (1-800-288-4677)

ISBN: 978-1-4620-4867-0 (sc)
ISBN: 978-1-4620-4868-7 (ebk)

Printed in the United States of America

iUniverse rev. date: 10/14/2011

Dedicated In loving memory of my late Grandmother,
Mavis Harrington.
Her heritage lives on.
Sunrise: May 15,1918
Sunset: February 17, 2009

CONTENTS

Inspiration

First and foremost, I give homage to my Lord and Savior, Jesus Christ, who is the inspiration of my life. Wonders cease to amaze me, in how effortless His transformations are; with gratitude I am humbled in seeing the beauty in all of His works.

To my wonderful daughters, Shantavia and Alisia: watching you girls grow into the respectful, ambitious, independent, and beautiful young women that you are today has been an honor. I have been blessed with the gift of motherhood. I say this is a gift because being a parent comes with lots of challenges. The most important lesson I learned in being a mother was how to let go. Tears are rolling down my face even now, as I seek the words to express the peace and gratification I have found in knowing that I've done a great job, and trusting that my daughters and their future is safe in the hands of my Lord and Savior.

With that said, I must also acknowledge myself because at times I can be my worst critic. Today I'm inspired with the blessings seen and not seen in my life. They have given me structure and an open mind to create, and my aspirations are to motivate lives in a positive way. I articulate this aspiration through poetry and my vision of unity.

My mom and dad are the best parents in the world. Now, I am sure that many people feel that way about their parents, but let me be honest: I haven't always felt that way. I do know that I come from a loving family, and the foundation of everything has to start with love. A parent's job is to guide and to provide the best upbringing that he or she can, and those are the gifts my parents gave me. When you're young and growing into adulthood, you don't always appreciate that. Today I would like to say this: I love you, Mommy and Daddy, and I thank you for all your encouragement. I love how you always respect each other and live your lives in harmony. That is the best way to describe how your relationship inspires me. I can always leave the troubles of the world behind me. You are my safe haven, and I admire you both for who you are.

I am the rose of Shar'-on, and the lily of the valleys. As the lily among thorns, so is my love among the daughters.
Songs of Solomon 2: 1-2 (The Message)

Introduction

I've traveled a road where there is no shame. Shouts: of slanderous remarks. Women being called out of their names, selling their souls short for this thing called fame. When did the gift of life become riddled into a puzzle, twisted into a game? This mockery is degrading, stereotypically berating. Who's to blame?

I am appalled that such a derogatory word has been embraced by the mainstream of our society. That "B word"—haven't you heard? It's a hip thing! Did you ever stop to think that the negative energy from this word would cause such a significant impact that it is now considered "politically correct" to refer to a woman—or anyone, for that matter—as the B word?

The English dictionary now has new definitions applied to the word B***H. It is no longer just a female dog; the second definition is now "a spiteful woman," and the third newly accepted definition is "a difficult and unpleasant person." It is a sad thing because millions of people embrace the word as being acceptable without knowing this information. Now at the end of the day no one really wants to be called this word. It causes conflict and animosity, but most of all, it is a hurtful word. Words are very powerful, and if they are not used in the right way, they can trigger negative and spiteful sentiments.

I have used the last letter of the word, H, to emphasize the word "her" at the beginning of each motif. Then I follow with a positive message that focuses on women's finer qualities.

We, as women, need to take a stance for ourselves. We need to be mindful of the words we say and demand the level of respect that we deserve, and want to attain. If we look in our mirrors and identify our good qualities, we will see ourselves for the phenomenal women that God created us to be. The poems, motifs, and photos in this book illustrate inspirational views of how the pure essence of a woman's worth should be valued. Of course, this is my opinion, but I speak on behalf of women of all nationalities to say, do you value you? We walk many paths in life, and we have many words to live by, but these four are essential: self-respect, self-love, self-worth, and self-esteem. Own them. Embrace them. Exude them!

A wholesome tongue is a tree of life:
but perverseness therein is a breach in the spirit.
Proverbs 15:4 (The Message)

Motivation

Eye See Unity was created for the sole purpose of bringing about unity and positivity, strengths that are so needed in our society today. My vision comes from an inner zeal to find the beauty in any situation. Not often does the desire to find beauty come about right away, but through patience and time, it's evident to me that the simplicities of life can bring much joy to difficult circumstances.

I am a mother of two beautiful young women, and my responsibility as a parent has always been to set the tone of love, respect, security, and guidance. I use the word "beautiful" often in my poetry because that's where I am today—in a beautiful place—and I have God to thank for that.

My motivation is to inspire women nationwide by promoting self-respect, self-love, self-worth, and building self-esteem, especially among our younger generation. We should never subject ourselves to any form of disrespect. What it is to be a woman is greater than we could ever imagine. The nature of being a woman is to be caring, loving, and protective; to bring forth life and to guide that new life into a mature and responsible adulthood. This goal should always be validated because, without women, the human race simply would not go on.

> And she spake out with a loud voice, and said, Blessed art thou among women, and blessed is the fruit of thy womb.
> Luke 1: 42 (The Message)

Eye C Unity

We are women,
the embodiment of God's creation,
seeking affirmation without hesitation
in the continuation of this civilization,
abolishment of discrimination
throughout the nation,
anticipating the persuasion
respect due through affiliation.
Public communications
are far from admiration.
Reunite justice and divinity.
"Eye See the Unity,"
surpassed by the epitome
of you and me.
Let the residue flock on
from here to eternity.
Peace rock on.

I Surrender

The woman in me
surrenders all, to fall
is not an option.
The dream is now in caption.
The clock ticks, and when it tocks,
I start clocking my surroundings.
Everything's out of order
that I'm watching.
Weathering the storms,
tackling the wrongs,
making things right:
this journey in life is not a fair fight,
but I'm determined, so I hold tight.
Hold up: I must be dreaming
because this battle is not my fight.

Confident

In all honesty,
the woman in me
cherishes what's mine
at this moment in time.
I've had an epiphany,
embracing this life with dignity.
I accept the good,
then I become greater.
With this, I know I must be better.

The Woman in Me

She blossoms like a flower,
bearing fruits sweet and sour
extending her limbs to a high tower,
sprouts of flourishing buds
nourished by the Son.
Nurtured beauty of this eloquent love,
purist of this quaint of essence One.
perfumed with an unfamiliar scent
of such extreme magnificence,
satisfying is this sanctifying burst of fulfillment.
It fills the air, fragranced in endearment:
sugarplums, spiced with a hint of honeysuckle
strummed from notes of amber soaked in my vanilla,
sweetened lips quenched by the aromas
of this long-lasting kiss.

Strength

The woman in me
is respectfully grateful,
strong, beautiful, humbled,
and faithful.
I kneel, and I pray, for today is
a new day.
I move forward, avoiding
obstacles that may
stand In my way.

Relevé

I may have stumbled,
did not fall
in the beauty
of it all,
uplifted in a higher call.
The focus is clearly
on you, my Lord.
What it is to be reborn?
Transformed, crucified, resurrected.
Cannot lie:
it wasn't easy, still not easy.
Can you feel me?
Please believe me
when I tell you I survived.

Her Clever

Her
Clever
Theories
Invokes
Brilliance

Ascended

On the inside looking out,
I reinforce my clout.
I'm on my grind, no doubt.
Looking up to the sky
with my head held high,
feeling like the greatest:
why shouldn't I?

I'm Thankful

I've been through the fire,
though I didn't get burnt.
The blaze was hot.
Many lessons are learnt.
Getting it right, here on this earth:
the pearls uprooted;
I'm about to give birth.
Resurrecting in the Trinity,
pour it out to the community:
"Eye See Unity"
in the eye of the beholder. Beauty,
manifest to the outreach,
inner love that can teach.
Many are lost, so I reach.

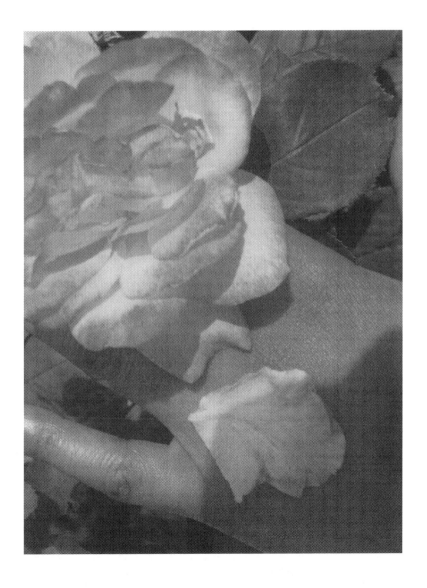

Her Cherished

Her
Cherished
Testimonies
Increase
Blessings

Conqueror

The woman in me,
is more than a conqueror.
I rise above all infirmities,
overlooking the proximity.
Many a days of indignities
I rise above, for these are the
powers that be.
Knocking them off like blocks,
in a domino effect:
flee from me.
Don't hinder my connect.
Tearing down strongholds
Metamorphically, He protects.
I rise above in the midst of this process.

Purify

The woman in me
is an important vessel.
My daily duty is to love,
honor, and cherish this temple.

Discipline

The woman in me
would like to achieve
goals that may be at a far reach.
Sacrificing my external wants
and protecting my internal needs
instills in me the ability to
accomplish my each and every dream.

Courageous at Heart

The woman in me
is courageous indeed,
living my life more abundantly
assertive, and outspokenly:
direct and carefree.

Faith

The woman in me
looks past what I can see,
knowing that there is
a significant purpose in me
being myself and not what others
expect of me:
manifested in faith,
walking in prosperity.

His Purpose

The woman in me
tends to seek and define
what's different, unique
genuine, and divine.
At the end of the day,
it doesn't matter what you say.
I know it's not all about me anyway.

Her Creativity

Her
Creativity
Transpires
Impeccable
Bliss

Tranquility

The woman in me
is righteously refined
sentimental, and kind,
graced with a love that lasts
until the end of time.

Believe in Yourself

The woman in me
can master my dreams
by making them become my
reality.

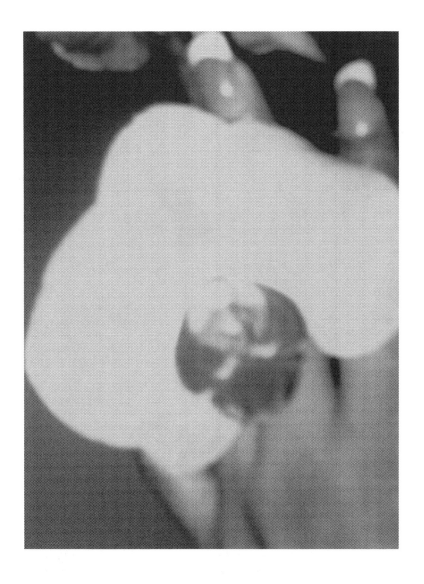

Affirmed

The woman in me
can achieve anything
as long as I have
a dream and a pen,
inspired by making
a difference with good intent,
taking a stance without any regrets.

Serenity

The woman in me,
sober and clean,
lending my life
with such purity,
established in the
grace of His serenity,
which invokes a natural stability.

Her Charisma

Her
Charisma
Transcends
Integrity
Boldly

Her Compelling

Her
Compelling
Teachings
Intrigue
Billions

Volume

The woman in me
is on this journey,
sustained in beliefs
of anticipated liberties,
challenged in confidence,
rugged around her edge
stepping up to the plate:
ready, get steady, now escalate.

Her Courageous

Her
Courageous
Topics
Inspires
Beings

Her Couture

**Her
Couture
Trends
Illuminates
Brides**

This Is Me

The woman in me
is born for the challenge.
I do manage to do damage
for all the haters
who can't stand this;
just know that
I'm far from average.

Her Classy

Her
Classy
Terrific
Impulse
Blossoms

Assured

The woman in me
elevates with preparation,
pressing on
in extreme motivation.

It's My Time to Shine

The woman in me
holds on to what's dear,
searching for the beloved
for many years.
Geared In headlights,
keen in eyesight:
battle no more,
walking in His might.
Adding up everything
from the beginning:
the score is even
in the ninth inning.
Back up, because
I'm going through winning.

Joyful

The woman in me
happy, silly, and playful.
Curious am I,
understanding and noble.

On Point

The woman in me
savvy, sweet, and sassy.
On the flipside,
I regulate those who harass me.

Her Curvaceous

Her
Curvaceous
Torso
Illustrates
Bossy

Greatness

The woman in me
has likes and dislikes.
What I've discovered is not to focus
on the negative, build on the positive,
evaluate and reciprocate,
gain strengths from equality,
eliminate volatile boundaries.
This bothers me.
My credence holds steadfast in ideology.
As I emancipate
Things that may encumber me,
I rest in assurance,
for it is He who is molding me.

Her Confidence

Her
Confidence
Truly
Incorporates
Business

You and I

The woman in me
takes walks on the beach,
replenishing my soul.
To teach one I preach
Standing strong,
I do beseech Thee,
Early in the morn He greets me.
Sunrise and sunsets:
on the horizon,
Thin eyes are kept.
I exhale, confined by the breeze.
Drawing me close
I'm holding my peace,
as the wind kissed mine ear,
leaving me at ease.

The Gift

The woman in me
Is reminiscent of the joys of life:
souls that are meek,
enlightened without strife.

Her Corporation

Her
Corporation
Tributes
Innovative
Brands

Love

The woman in me
has a love that is fearless,
peacefully refined,
mellow and unselfish,
subjected to humilities,
ridiculed in every proximity.
Still, in the midst I stay
true to this:
cherished in this eternal gift.

Her Cosmetology

**Her
Cosmetology
Technique
Is
Brilliant**

Jesus

The woman in me
believes that, out of all the
billions of molecules created:
Stars, Neptune, Venus, and Uranus,
there is one that shines the brightest,
assuring me of the King, He's righteous.

Her Colorful

Her
Colorful
Thrilling
Image
Brightens

Create Peace

The woman in me
has goals to achieve,
setting me apart
to create a work of art
that may generate
the fortified elements, unified,
facilitating those lost and fallen
by the wayside.
So if we see love, we can be love
by keeping hope alive.

Triumphant and True

The woman in me
must always be brave,
never giving the impression
of being doubtful or afraid,
upright in her posture,
affirmed in her character,
trusting, because I'm neither
nor the narrator.

The Vision

The woman in me
enjoys the vision of beautiful things.
Everything I touch has purpose,
clutched in remembrance
of such discerning gratitude.
Oh, how I long to burst and erupt
with joy in a vision that may heal
a girl or a boy.

Her Cute

Her
Cute
Tenderness
Irresistibly
Blooms

Discover the Dance

The woman in me
loves to dance and plié,
do twirls and splits, and even ballet.
Tip-toe hurray, tip-toe hurray!
The woman in me loves to dance and plié,
arise with poise as I extend my relevé.

Cold but Nice

The woman in me
is no longer in darkness.
My instincts are clear,
temptations are farthest.
I reap what I sow,
so bountiful is my harvest.
I work on this daily
so I can say clearly:
there is no mystery.
The victimized is history
cold as ice, cold as ice:
The woman in me can be
cold, but nice.
Her spices are sweet as treats,
rotten to the teeth.
Who spoiled her?
A woman so cold,
bet, yet no one owns her.
She hurts to the bone.
Selfless love jones her.
Hurt no more, hurt no more.
Freeze this pain on hot ice
and hurt no more.

Her Character

Her
Character
Tangibly
Influences
Bachelors

Celebration

The woman in me
has a golden dream:
to lose,
never is that an option for me,
so I takes one for the team.
The Lord has given me the ball;
victory and challenges
are a long haul.
I'm in His court now,
eliminating distractions,
going in on the rebound.
Best believe the ref has placed his bet.
Taking it home,
now I'm off the bench,
looking both ways, so now I check.
I assume the position as I eject:
ready, aim, fire,
and guess what's next?
Victory is mine;
shrug it off, 'cause I'm blessed.

Step to This

Eye C Unity:
look with your eyes
and tell me what you see.
The woman in me is phenomenally
great, that's what I be.
H to the C to the T I B,
look with your eyes
and tell me what you see.
Her
Compassion
Triumphantly
Intercedes
Blessings
No more stressing:
it's time to stop disrespecting.
We are definitely not the definition
of that B word,
so tell me what you heard.
Had to put a swerve on it,
I put a curve on it.
Watch your tongue.
Lessons: learn from it.

Beautiful Art the Rose

Beautiful art the rose that is she.
Soft and delicate as a flower,
developed and refined by the hour,
authentic and exquisitely showered.
As each petal falls to the ground,
seasons preserve her
till she comes back around.
Her savour lingered with a dignified valor.
Time pieced together this graceful flower.

Perseverance

There's a lion and a bear in all of us.
Tap into it, contain it,
then soar like an eagle.
Settle like a dove.
Rest in assurance,
balanced in His love.
After all, we're only human,
enduring the humanities
of strengths that live through us.
Those that are granted supernaturally.
Purify your heart; reflections of Thee.

Woman

The struggle of being a woman
is like a beating drum;
her rhythmic moods grow tiresome.
Struck by each element
of her eloquent thrust,
in her sophistication there is lust.
The clacking of her footsteps when she struts
toward each moment of life, eager to trust,
fulfilled in excitement,
perplexed in delightment.
What is it that she searches for?
An essential extension of her preference galore.
Need I say more?

Logical

You've got to crawl before you fall,
stand strong before you walk.
People crumble when they stumble
over words, if they're not humbled.
What it is to live shall be,
and what is not will supersede.

Charisma

Charismatic as she danced those acrobatic moves through life,
her high-society beams of lights, camera, action, a star-studded
perfection,
the glimmer of her shimmer milkens her silken skin.
Zoom in on a whim if you could get it in.
Drenched with earth tones soaked deep within,
tanned and ripened, flawless to the Mohican.
Sun silhouettes down her back,
setting off shades of her bronzed aphrodisiac.
Glance if you get a chance
to captivate her enhanced beauty.
This here is a true woman about her duty:
multifaceted, profiling, and sure-nuff styling.
Her brilliance is far more amazing
than anyone who can get the job done.
Hats off: she's number one.

I C UNITY

The woman in me is authentically reserved.
My attributes are of esteemed satisfactions, preserved.
I fuse amongst the elite, unifying the realist and the obsoletes.
Altogether amused in versatile qualities, call it unique.
My creativity stems from the ambivalence
of our environment's un-equivalence.
I challenge myself every day that I awake,
acknowledging that I'm blessed,
and, no, this is not a risk that I take.
A divine appointment, set up with no debate.
No longer can I be considered mediocre.
I must step my game up,
meeting the objective of this quota.
It's not what I do,
it's what I oughta.
Blending this love of my persona,
remaining humble because I am the owner
by every means, arms strong in on this team:
I C Unity.

To all my readers, I give special thanks for your support, and God bless you. I never want to leave anyone out of anything that I am passionate about. I am genuinely reaching out to women because we are a very delicate part of the species, and I feel that a little more recognition should be addressed on how that is perceived. The fact remains that I am a woman, and my thoughts are relatable.

I want to include the guys in the *Eye C Unity* project. I am working on some phrases for the male gender in regards to the turnaround of the B word. Here is one of them.

His
Championship
Towers
Integrity
Bravely